Vegetarian

recipes from around the world

Sue Townsend and Caroline Young

Heinemann Library
Chicago, Illinois

© 2003 Heinemann Library
a division of Reed Elsevier Inc.
Chicago, Illinois

Customer Service 888-454-2279

Visit our website at
www.heinemannlibrary.com

Designed by Jo Hinton-Malivoire and
Tinstar Design Limited (www.tinstar.co.uk)
Originated by Dot Gradations Ltd
Printed in China
by Wing King Tong

07 06 05 04 03
10 9 8 7 6 5 4 3 2 1

**Library of Congress Cataloging-in-
Publication Data**
Townsend, Sue, 1963-
   Vegetarian recipes from around the world /
by Sue Townsend and Caroline Young.
      p. cm. -- (A world of recipes)
Summary: Presents a collection of meatless
recipes from around the world, including
walnut, fenugreek and yogurt soup from Iran,
apple pancakes from the Netherlands, and
pineapple curry from Sri Lanka. Also
discusses the growing popularity of
vegetarianism and how to maintain a
balanced diet.
Includes bibliographical references and index.
   ISBN 1-4034-0977-3 (hardcover) -- ISBN 1-
4034-3653-3 (pbk.)
  1. Vegetarian cookery--Juvenile literature. 2.
Cookery,
International--Juvenile literature. [1.
Vegetarian cookery. 2. Cookery,
International.] I. Young, Caroline, 1939- II.
Title.
   TX837.T69 2003
   641.5'636--dc21

2002155854

Acknowledgments
The author and publishers are grateful to the
following for permission to reproduce
copyright material: p. 6 Corbis; all other
photographs Gareth Boden.

Cover photographs reproduced with
permission of Gareth Boden.

Every effort has been made to contact
copyright holders of any material reproduced
in this book. Any omissions will be rectified in
subsequent printings if notice is given to the
publisher.

Some words are shown in
bold, **like this.** You can find
out what they mean by
looking in the glossary.

Contents

Key

* easy

** medium

*** difficult

Vegetarian Food

Many people in the world are **vegetarian**. This means that they do not eat any meat. Some vegetarians eat fish, but no meat. Other vegetarians, called **vegans**, do not eat any food that has come from an animal, including milk and eggs. Instead of dairy products, they may eat foods made with soy milk, which is made from soybeans. Whatever people eat, it is important to make sure that their body is getting the **nutrients** it needs.

Is it healthy to be a vegetarian?

Animal foods, such as meat, fish, and eggs contain **protein**, which our bodies need to stay healthy. Fruits, **legumes**, and vegetables do not have as much protein as animal foods, but eating a wide range of them will give you all the protein you need. Below are some foods that vegetarians eat.

squash

cabbage

pineapple

rutabaga

peas

lemon

red peppers

potatoes

yogurt

sweet corn

apples

carrots

onion

turnips

garlic

ginger

pecans

bread

cheese

beans

leeks

cinnamon

Legumes

Legumes are beans and seeds from plants. They include kidney beans, black-eyed beans, and chickpeas. Legumes are a very good source of protein and can be cooked in many different ways. You can buy most legumes dried or canned.

Nuts

Nuts, such as walnuts, pecans, and peanuts, are another good source of protein. Many cooking styles around the world use nuts in sweet and tasty recipes. Nuts contain a lot of fat, so do not eat too many.

Dairy or soy products

Milk, cheese, and yogurt are dairy products. They contain protein and **calcium**, which help give us strong bones and teeth. Vegans can get calcium from dairy substitutes, such as soy milk with added calcium. Grocery stores sell both types of products.

Fruits and vegetables

Fruits and vegetables are a good source of **vitamins**, which everyone needs to stay healthy. You can buy many different kinds of fruits and vegetables in grocery stores. They come from all over the world. Dried fruits, and canned and frozen fruits and vegetables contain nutrients, too.

Grains

Around the world, people eat rice every day. It is a **staple** ingredient in many countries. People also eat other grains, such as wheat and barley. Health-food stores sell a variety of grains, including bulgur wheat.

Around the World

There are more **vegetarians** today than there have ever been, and their numbers are growing. There are several reasons why people choose not to eat meat.

Why are people vegetarian?

In poorer parts of the world, people may have no choice about being vegetarian. Meat is a luxury food that they cannot afford. Some families keep a cow, goat, or chicken for their milk or their eggs, but their animal is too valuable to kill for meat.

Many millions of people avoid eating meat for religious reasons. The followers of Hinduism and Buddhism, for example, believe that they should respect all living beings and live in a way that does not cause any harm. Because of this, many are vegetarians.

▶ *A wide variety of vegetables are being sold at this market stall in India.*

Other vegetarians have made a choice not to eat meat. They believe that it is wrong to **breed** and kill other living things for our food. Many people feel that they will enjoy better health if they follow a vegetarian diet, so they do not eat meat.

The vegetarian world

There are vegetarians in every part of the world. The recipes in this book come from all around the world. The map below shows you where the countries that the recipes come from are located.

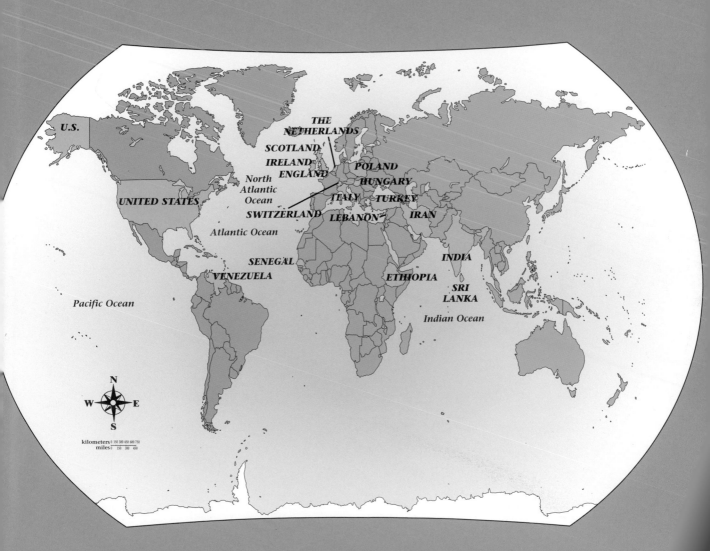

Before You Start

Kitchen rules

There are a few basic rules you should always follow when you are cooking:

- Ask an adult if you can use the kitchen.
- Some cooking processes, especially those involving hot water or oil, can be dangerous. When you see this sign, take extra care or ask an adult to help.
- Wash your hands before you start.
- Wear an apron to protect your clothes.
- Be very careful when you use sharp knives.
- Never leave pan handles sticking out because you might bump into them and spill hot food.
- Always use oven mitts to lift things in and out of the oven.
- Wash fruits and vegetables before you use them.
- Always wash chopping boards very well after use, especially after chopping raw meat, fish, or poultry.
- Use a separate chopping board for onions and garlic, if possible.

How long will it take?

Some of the recipes in this book are quick and easy, and some are more difficult and take longer. The stripe across the right-hand side of each recipe page tells you how long it takes to prepare a dish from start to finish. It also shows how difficult each recipe is to make: * (easy), ** (medium), or *** (difficult).

Quantities and measurements

You can see how many people each recipe will serve at the top of each right-hand page. You can multiply or divide the quantities if you want to cook for more or fewer people.

Ingredients for recipes can be measured in two ways. Imperial measurements use cups and ounces. Metric measurements use grams and milliliters.

In the recipes, you will see the following abbreviations:

tbsp = tablespoon	oz = ounce	cm = centimeter
tsp = teaspoon	lb = pound	g = gram
ml = milliliter	l = liter	in. = inch

Utensils

To cook the recipes in this book, you will need these utensils (as well as essentials, such as spoons, plates, and bowls):

- plastic or glass chopping board (easier to clean than wooden ones)
- food processor or blender
- large frying pan
- 9-in. (23-cm) heavy-based non-stick frying pan
- measuring cup
- colander
- small and large saucepans, with lids
- set of scales

- sharp knife
- slotted spoon
- kitchen spatula
- baking sheets
- lemon squeezer
- potato masher
- apple corer
- whisk
- 8-in. (20-cm) plate
- pastry brush

 Whenever you use kitchen knives, be very careful.

Fava Bean Pâté with Ciabatta Toast (Italy)

There are many **vegetarian** recipes from Italy. This one is from Tuscany, an area famous both for its old towns and cities and for its beautiful countryside. This recipe uses frozen fava beans, because fresh ones are only available for a short time each year. Ciabatta (pronounced *chee-a-batta*) is a type of Italian bread, which you can find in many grocery stores or bakeries. Serve the pâté with some salad as an ideal starter, light lunch, or snack.

What you need

1 onion
3 garlic cloves
2 tbsp olive oil
14 oz (400 g) frozen fava beans
2½ oz (70 g) reduced-fat cream cheese
1 lemon
1 ciabatta loaf

What you do

1 **Peel** and finely **chop** the onion and garlic.

(!) 2 Heat the oil in a small frying pan over a medium heat. **Fry** the onion and garlic for 5 minutes, until they are softened. Leave them to cool.

(!) 3 Put the frozen fava beans into a saucepan and cover them with water. Bring the water to a **boil**, cover the pan, and **simmer** the beans for 5 minutes.

4 **Drain** the beans and let them cool.

5 Put them into a food processor or blender. Add the cream cheese and the fried onion mixture.

6 Cut the lemon in half. Using a lemon squeezer, squeeze the juice from both halves.

7 Add the lemon juice to the bean mixture, and **blend** until smooth.

8 Using a spatula, scrape the pâté into a bowl for serving.

9 Cut the ciabatta into 1-in. (2½-cm) thick slices. **Toast** the slices of bread on each side until lightly browned.

10 Serve the ciabatta warm with the pâté and a salad.

Walnut, Fenugreek, and Yogurt Soup (Iran)

For hundreds of years, Iran was in the middle of trading routes between Europe and Asia. Iran's cooking style has been influenced by the many different people who have visited the country throughout history. In Iran, this soup is served hot or cold, as a starter or light lunch. It contains the **ground** seeds of a plant called fenugreek. Fenugreek leaves can be added to salads, too.

What you need

1 onion
1 tbsp vegetable oil or butter
2 oz (50 g) walnuts
1 tsp ground fenugreek
2½ cups (600 ml) water
1 tbsp cornstarch
2¼ cups (520 ml) plain yogurt

What you do

1 **Peel** and finely **chop** the onion.

2 Heat the oil or butter in a saucepan over medium heat. Add the onion and **fry** over medium to low heat for 4–5 minutes, until it has softened.

3 Put the walnuts into a blender, and **blend** until finely chopped. Add the walnuts and fenugreek to the saucepan.

4 In a bowl, stir 4 tbsp of the water into the cornstarch.

5 Add the rest of the water to the pan. **Cover** and **simmer** for 20 minutes, and then allow to cool for 5 minutes.

(!) **6** Stir the yogurt into the cornstarch mixture. Add 8 oz (237 ml) of the liquid from the saucepan to the yogurt mixture, and stir well.

7 Slowly pour the yogurt mixture into the pan, stirring all the time. Reheat the soup, but do not let it **boil**. Serve hot or cold with some bread.

MAKING YOGURT

To make your own yogurt, heat 2¼ cups (520 ml) of milk until it is just boiling. Let it cool until it is warm, then stir in 2 tbsp plain yogurt. Pour into a clean jar and keep in a warm place for 6–8 hours, until set. **Chill** the yogurt for 12 hours before serving.

Black-Eyed Bean Cakes (Ethiopia)

Farmers in north and central African countries, such as Ethiopia, grow black-eyed beans, or black-eyed peas, as they are sometimes called. African cooks usually soak the beans, pour them into a bowl, and **mash** them with a simple stone or wooden tool. They **deep-fry** their bean cakes, but this version fries them in a little oil.

What you need

7 oz (200 g) dried black-eyed beans
A 6 oz (150 g) sweet potato
1 onion
Pinch of salt
Half of a red chili pepper (if you like them)
1 tbsp flour
3 tbsp oil

What you do

1 Put the black-eyed beans into a bowl, and cover them with cold water. Soak them overnight.

2 **Drain** the beans. Rub them between your hands so that the skins come off. Put them into a bowl and rinse the skins away by pouring water over them.

3 **Peel** the sweet potato and cut it into 1-in. (2½-cm) chunks. Peel and finely **chop** the onion.

4 Put the potato into a saucepan, cover it with **boiling** water, and add a pinch of salt. Cook for 15 minutes, or until it is tender, and then drain it.

5 Cut the half of a chili pepper in half lengthwise and throw away the seeds. Chop the chili pepper finely. Wash your hands thoroughly after handling chili peppers. The juice can irritate your eyes and skin.

6 Put the beans into a blender. Add the onion and pepper, and **blend** until smooth. Add the potato and blend again.

7 Sprinkle a little of the flour onto a work surface. Take out 2 tbsp of the mixture, and shape it into a ball. Then flatten it into a round shape. Do this with the rest of the mixture, to make about 20 fritters.

(!) 8 Heat the oil in a large frying pan over medium heat. **Fry** the bean cakes, four or five at a time, for 4 minutes on each side, until golden. Lift the cooked bean cakes onto paper towels.

9 Serve immediately, with cooked, green vegetables or salad, as a starter or light lunch.

Gobi Paratha (India)

Many people in India are **vegetarian**. They cook different dishes using vegetables and **legumes**. In India, people often scoop up their food with flat breads, such as parathas. This recipe is for a paratha stuffed with vegetables. Parathas can also be flavored with spices or fried onion.

What you need

3 oz (100 g) cauliflower florets

1 tsp salt

1 onion

Quarter of a green chili pepper (if you like them)

1-in. (2½-cm) piece fresh ginger

1 tbsp fresh coriander (chopped)

11 oz (300 g) whole wheat flour

¾ cup water

4 tbsp ghee (clarified butter) or vegetable oil

What you do

1 **Chop** or **grate** the cauliflower florets finely, into very small pieces. Pour them into a colander over the sink. Sprinkle them with some salt, and leave to **drain** for 30 minutes.

2 Meanwhile, **peel** and finely chop the onion.

3 Cut the piece of pepper in half, and throw away the seeds. Chop the pepper finely. Wash your hands after touching raw pepper.

4 Peel and grate the ginger. Rinse the cauliflower pieces and pat them dry.

5 Put the cauliflower, onion, chili pepper, ginger, and coriander into a bowl, and stir well.

6 Put the flour into a bowl, add 2 tbsp ghee or vegetable oil, and a pinch of salt. Stir in ¾ cup (200 ml) of water. Using your hands, make the mixture into a stiff dough.

7 Sprinkle a little flour on a work surface. Stretch the dough, fold it over, then press it with the palm of your hand. Turn it round by one-quarter, and repeat. **Knead** it in this way for 3 minutes.

8 Cut the dough into four pieces. Using a rolling pin, roll each one out to form a 6-in. (15-cm) circle. Brush a little ghee or oil over each.

9 Scatter the cauliflower mixture over the circles. Gather each circle up to make a ball. Carefully roll each ball out into a 9-in. (23-cm) circle.

⊘ 10 Brush each paratha with a little ghee or oil. Heat a heavy-based frying pan over medium heat. **Fry** each paratha for 3–4 minutes on each side, until golden brown.

11 Serve warm with pineapple curry (page 36), **chutney**, and rice.

Barley and Vegetable Soup (Poland)

Winters in Poland can be extremely cold, so warm, filling soups such as this one are a popular lunch or dinner meal. Polish farmers grow the vegetables this soup contains, as well as many different kinds of fruit. They bottle fruits or make it into jam, before **exporting** it to other countries.

What you need

3 oz (75 g) pearl barley
6 cups (1½ l) hot water
1 carrot
1 parsnip
2 potatoes
1 celery stick
2 onions
2 tbsp vegetable oil
2 oz (50 g) button
   mushrooms
2 vegetable stock cubes
Salt and pepper

What you do

1 Put the pearl barley into a bowl and cover it with cold water. Leave it to soak for 4 hours.

2 **Drain** the barley. Put it into a pan, add half the hot water, and bring it to the **boil. Cover** the pan and **simmer** for 30 minutes.

3 **Peel** the carrot and parsnip, and trim off both ends. Peel the potatoes.

4 Cut all three vegetables into ½-in. (1-cm) slices, and then into cubes.

5 Trim the ends off the celery. Cut it into ½-in. (1-cm) pieces.

6 Peel and **chop** the onions.

(!) 7 Heat the oil in a large saucepan over a medium heat. **Fry** the onion for 3 minutes, or until it is softened. Add the celery, potato, carrot, and parsnip. Stir well. Cook for 5 minutes, stirring occasionally.

8 **Slice** the mushrooms thinly and add them to the pan.

(!) 9 Add the pearl barley and the cooking liquid. Pour in the rest of the hot water.

10 Crumble the stock cubes into the pan, stirring well. Bring to a boil, cover, and simmer for 20 minutes.

11 Add a pinch of salt and pepper. Spoon the soup into bowls. Serve with crusty bread.

Chickpeas with Sugar Snap Peas (Senegal)

Many traditional African dishes are made in one pot, hung over a fire. All the ingredients are cooked together as a complete meal, as in this recipe from Senegal, in northwest Africa. Sugar snap peas are grown throughout Africa.

What you need

1 onion

1 garlic clove

1 lb (450 g) sugar snap peas

2 tomatoes

1 tbsp vegetable oil

1 tsp black mustard seeds

1 tsp **ground** cumin

14-oz (400-g) can chickpeas

What you do

1 **Peel** and finely **chop** the onion and garlic.

2 Cut the ends off the sugar snap peas and cut them in half.

3 Chop the tomatoes.

(!) 4 Heat the oil in a medium saucepan over a medium heat. Add the onion and garlic, and **fry** for 3 minutes, or until they are softened.

5 Stir in the sugar snap peas and tomatoes, and cook for 5 minutes.

6 Add the mustard seeds and cumin. Cook for 1 minute.

7 Empty the chickpeas into a colander. Rinse them under cold running water.

8 Stir the chickpeas into the sugar snap peas mixture. **Cover** the pan and cook for 4–5 minutes, until steaming hot.

9 Spoon onto a serving dish. Serve immediately.

Colcannon (Ireland)

For centuries, potatoes were a **staple** food in Ireland. If the potato harvest failed, many people starved. Colcannon is a traditional dish that mixes potatoes with green onions and cabbage. If it is served at Halloween, a silver coin or charm is sometimes stirred into the mixture—whoever gets the charm is predicted to marry within a year.

What you need

1½ lbs (750 g)
  potatoes
Pinch of salt
Half a bunch of green
  onions
4 oz (100 g) cabbage
½ cup (100 ml) milk
¼ cup (50 g) butter

What you do

1 **Peel** the potatoes and cut them into 1½-in. (4-cm) chunks. Put them into a pan with a pinch of salt.

(!) 2 Cover the potatoes with **boiling** water. Bring the water back to a boil, **cover**, and **simmer** for 17 minutes (you may want to set a timer for this).

3 Trim the ends off the green onions and throw them away. Cut the green onions into thin slices.

4 Wash the cabbage and **chop** it into small pieces.

5 Add the onions and the cabbage to the potatoes in the pan, and cook for 3 minutes more.

6 Carefully **drain** the potatoes, onions, and cabbage into a colander, and then put them back into the hot pan.

7 **Mash** the vegetables with a potato masher. Add enough milk to make a light, fluffy mixture.

8 Stir in half the butter, and some salt and pepper to taste.

9 Put the colcannon into a serving dish. Make several dips in the top with a teaspoon and put a little bit of the remaining butter into each dip. Serve hot, with other vegetables.

Olive, Pomegranate, and Walnut Salad (Turkey)

Summers are very hot in Turkey, so people there usually eat a light lunch. They eat their main meal in the evening, when it is cooler. This recipe is from southeastern Turkey, where farmers grow all the ingredients—olives, walnuts, and pomegranates.

What you need

1 pomegranate
2 oz (50 g) fresh coriander
1 bunch green onions
¾ cup (120 g) walnuts
1 oz (25 g) fresh sorrel or spinach leaves
1¼ cups (120 g) Queen green olives

*For the **dressing**:*
3 tbsp olive oil
1½ tbsp lemon juice
Salt and pepper

What you do

1 Cut the pomegranate in half. Hold each half skin-side up over a bowl, and tap it with a spoon or rolling pin so that the seeds drop into the bowl.

2 **Chop** the coriander finely.

3 Trim the ends off the spring onions and throw them away. Cut the spring onions into thin slices.

4 Put the walnuts into a blender and **blend** until roughly chopped.

5 Rinse the sorrel or spinach leaves under cold running water, and pat them dry with a clean paper towel. Cut off the tough stalks.

6 Put all the dressing ingredients into a small screw-topped jar.

7 Shake together all the salad ingredients in a bowl. Shake the dressing well, pour it over the salad, and toss again.

8 Spoon the salad onto individual plates, and serve with crusty bread.

OLIVES

Olives grow on trees in groups called groves. Some olive trees can produce olives for up to 300 years. The olives are harvested and soaked in saltwater for eating, or crushed to make olive oil.

Sweet Corn, Pepper, and Pumpkin Stew (Venezuela)

Cooking all the ingredients for a meal in the same pot is part of traditional cooking in Venezuela, South America. Serve this vegetable stew as a main meal with crusty bread or rice.

What you need

2 onions

1 garlic clove

14 oz (400 g) pumpkin or butternut squash

2 ears corn on the cob, **thawed** if frozen

4 tomatoes

1 red pepper

4 small to medium potatoes

2 tbsp vegetable oil

3½ oz (100 g) peas, fresh or frozen

1 tbsp fresh chopped marjoram

2 cups (460 ml) water

What you do

1 **Peel** and finely **chop** the onions and garlic.

2 Peel the pumpkin or butternut squash. Throw away the seeds and cut flesh into 1-in. (2½-cm) chunks.

3 If using fresh corn on the cob, pull the leaves and silky threads off.

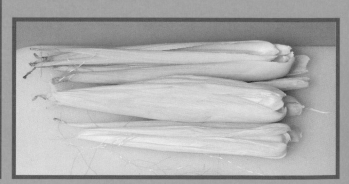

4 Cut the tomatoes into quarters. Cut the pepper in half, and throw away the stalk and seeds. Cut the flesh into 1-in. (2½-cm) pieces.

5 Peel the potatoes and cut them into 1-in. (2½-cm) chunks.

(!) **6** Heat the oil in a flameproof casserole dish or large pan over medium heat. **Fry** the onion for 3 minutes, add the garlic, and fry for 1 minute more.

7 Add the rest of the prepared vegetables, marjoram, salt, and pepper, and 2 cups (460 ml) of water to the pan. **Cover** and **simmer** for 25–30 minutes.

8 Using a slotted spoon, lift the sweet corn onto a cutting board. When it is cool, cut it into 1-in. (2½-cm) thick slices.

9 Add the sweet corn and peas to the pan, and cook for 5 minutes. Stir the stew, and spoon it into a serving dish (if you cooked it in a pan). Serve hot.

Tabbouleh (Lebanon)

Lebanon is in the Middle East, between Israel and Syria. Tabbouleh is a traditional Lebanese recipe, but people all over the Middle East make it. They may change some of the ingredients, depending on what is available locally, but it always includes bulgur wheat. Serve it with **pita bread** or as a side salad.

What you need

6 oz (175 g) bulgur (or cracked) wheat
1 lemon
2 tbsp olive oil
One-quarter of a cucumber
2 green onions
6 cherry tomatoes
4 tbsp chopped fresh parsley
2 tbsp chopped fresh mint
2½ cups (600 ml) water
Salt and pepper

What you do

1 Put the bulgur wheat into a heatproof bowl. Pick out any small stones.

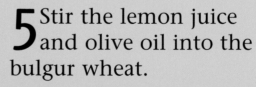

2 Pour 2½ cups (600 ml) **boiling** water over the wheat and stir well. Leave it for 30 minutes, stirring from time to time.

3 Put a colander over the sink and **drain** the wheat.

4 Cut the lemon in half. Using a lemon squeezer, squeeze the juice from both halves.

5 Stir the lemon juice and olive oil into the bulgur wheat.

6 Cut the cucumber into long slices ½-in. (1-cm) thick. Cut each slice into strips ½-in. (1-cm) thick. Cut across each strip to make ½-in. (1-cm) cubes.

7 Trim the ends off the green onions. Cut the green onions into ½-in. (1-cm) slices.

8 Cut the cherry tomatoes in half. Stir the chopped herbs and tomatoes into the bulgur wheat with the cucumber. Add some salt and pepper.

9 Serve immediately, with pita bread or crusty bread, or keep it in the refrigerator (it will keep for up to 2 days).

Winter Vegetable Goulash (Hungary)

In Hungary, winters are very cold and few things grow. Hungarians store vegetables in a dry, dark place, and cook them with tomatoes and a mild, red spice, paprika, to make this stew called goulash. Goulash can also have beans or meat as its main ingredient. Serve it as a main dish, with rice, pasta, or crusty bread.

What you need

2 onions
2 carrots
2 parsnips
7 oz (200 g) rutabaga
3½ oz (100 g) turnip
2 tbsp vegetable oil
1 tbsp paprika
2 tbsp plain flour
8 small new potatoes
14-oz (400-g) can chopped
   tomatoes
1 vegetable stock cube
2 tsp cornstarch
¾ cup (180 ml) sour
   cream
1¼ cups (300 ml) plus 2
   tbsp water

To garnish:
2 tbsp chopped
   fresh parsley

What you do

1 **Peel** and finely **chop** the onions.

2 Peel and **slice** the carrots and parsnips.

3 Peel the rutabaga and turnip. Cut them into 1-in. (2½-cm) thick slices, then into 1-in. chunks.

(!) 4 Heat the oil in a large saucepan. Add the onions and **fry** them for 3 minutes, until softened.

5 Stir in the chopped-up vegetables and paprika, and cook for 5 minutes, stirring from time to time.

6 Sprinkle the flour over the vegetables and cook for 1 minute, stirring all the time.

(!) 7 Pour 1¼ cups (300 ml) of **boiling** water over the vegetables. Add the potatoes and tomatoes.

8 Crumble the stock cube over the pan and stir well. **Cover** and **simmer** for 25 minutes.

9 In a cup, mix the cornstarch with 2 tbsp cold water. Stir the mixture into the sour cream, and then stir the cream into the vegetable mixture.

10 Carefully spoon the hot goulash onto a serving dish, and sprinkle with parsley to serve.

Cheese Fondue (Switzerland)

Sharing a fondue with friends is a popular Swiss tradition. Everyone takes turns to dip cubes of bread or vegetables into melted cheese in a fondue pan. A small burner under the pan keeps the cheese warm. If you do not have a **fondue set**, gently warm the ingredients in a heavy-based pan over a low heat on the stove. Keep the mixture warm by placing the pan over a heated dish warmer.

What you need

1 cup (200 ml) grape juice
1 tsp cornstarch
1 garlic clove
7 oz (200 g) Gruyère cheese
7 oz (200 g) Swiss cheese
1 French loaf (baguette)
4 thick slices rye bread
1 apple
2 tbsp lemon juice
2 carrots

What you do

1 Mix 2 tbsp of the grape juice with the cornstarch to make a smooth paste.

2 **Peel** and crush the garlic. Put it into the fondue pan with the cornstarch mixture and the remaining grape juice. Stir well.

3 Cut the rind off both the cheeses. Cut each piece into ½-in. (1-cm) thick slices, then ½-in. (1-cm) wide strips. Now cut the strips into ½-in. (1-cm) cubes.

4 **Slice** the baguette into 1-in. (2½-cm) slices, then cut each slice into quarters. Cut the rye bread into 1-in. (2½-cm) cubes.

5 Cut the apple into eight wedges. Cut out the core and throw away. Cut wedges into 1-in. (2½-cm) chunks. Put them in a bowl with the lemon juice.

6 Peel the carrots and cut them into 1-in. (2½-cm) chunks.

(!) **7** Ask an adult to light the fondue burner. Put the pan on top and let the mixture warm, but do not **boil**. Add the cheese, stirring until melted.

8 **Drain** the lemon juice from the apple. Put the apple, bread, and carrots on plates.

9 Give each person a fork (a long fondue fork, if you have it).

10 Each person, in turn, puts a piece of bread, apple or carrot on the fork, dips it into the cheese, stirs the mixture once, takes the fork out and eats! (Be careful: the melted cheese will be very hot.)

Vegetable Cornish Pasties (England)

Cornwall is in the far southwest of England. These filled pastry envelopes, called pasties, were first made as lunch for miners working deep in the Cornish tin mines. The men could not wash their hands before eating, so they held a pastry corner as they ate, then threw away the dirty part. Pasties are ideal as part of a picnic or as a lunch.

What you need

5 oz (125 g) potatoes
5 oz (125 g) carrots
5 oz (125 g) rutabaga
Half of a vegetable
    stock cube
1 onion
1 tbsp vegetable oil
1 tbsp flour
Thawed puff pastry
1 egg
Water

To garnish:
Sprigs of fresh parsley

What you do

1 **Peel** the potatoes, carrots, and rutabaga. Cut each into ½-in. (1-cm) slices, then into ½-in. cubes. Put vegetables into a saucepan.

2 Crumble in the half stock cube. **Cover** the vegetables with **boiling** water, and cook for 10 minutes.

3 Peel and finely **chop** the onion. Heat the oil in a small pan, and **fry** the onion over low to medium heat for 4 minutes.

4 **Drain** the potato, rutabaga, and carrots, and then add them to the onion. Leave them to cool completely.

5 **Preheat** the oven to 400°F (200°C). Sprinkle the flour on a work surface. Use a rolling pin to roll the pastry out until it is about ¼-in. (½-cm) thick.

6 Put an 8-in. (20-cm) plate on the pastry and cut around it. Repeat this to make six pastry circles.

7 Spoon the vegetables along the center of each circle. Keep them away from the edge.

8 Brush a little water around the circles' edges. Fold the pastry over the filling. Press the pastry edge between your fingers to make a zigzag ridge along the edge of each pasty.

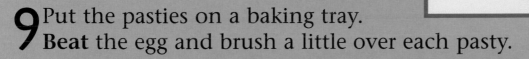

9 Put the pasties on a baking tray. **Beat** the egg and brush a little over each pasty.

10 **Bake** for 25 minutes, until golden. Let the pasties cool a little before eating them. Garnish with a sprig of parsley.

Pineapple Curry (Sri Lanka)

Sri Lanka is an island in the Indian Ocean, just off the southern tip of India. This recipe uses pineapples and coconuts, two of the island's main crops. It also uses the dried leaves of the curry plant, which add a spicy flavor. Use a heavy-based saucepan for this recipe, if you can. Sri Lankan cooks use a pot called a *chatty*.

What you need

One-quarter of a fresh chili pepper (if you like it)
1 tsp mustard seeds
1 shallot
1 large, ripe pineapple
One-quarter of a stem of lemongrass
1 tbsp vegetable oil
3 dried curry leaves
½ cup (100 ml) coconut milk
Pinch of saffron
1 small cinnamon stick
½ tsp **ground** cumin

What you do

1 **Chop** the quarter of a chili pepper finely (if you are using it), and then wash your hands thoroughly. Chili pepper juice can irritate your eyes and skin.

2 Put the mustard seeds into a small frying pan, and **dry-fry** them over a medium heat for 30 seconds, until they "pop." Pour them onto a plate.

3 **Peel** and finely chop the shallot.

4 Cut the pineapple in half. Cut off the thick skin and leaves, and throw them away. Cut out the tough core in the middle, and throw it away. Chop the flesh into 1-in. (2½-cm) chunks.

5 Peel off the outer leaves off the lemongrass. Trim off the root end and throw it away. Finely chop the lemongrass.

(!) 6 Heat the oil in a saucepan over medium heat. **Fry** the shallot for 1 minute. Add the lemon grass and curry leaves, and fry for 1 minute.

7 Stir in the coconut milk and all the other ingredients, except the ground cumin. **Simmer** for 10 minutes, stirring from time to time.

8 Stir in the cumin, and simmer for 5 minutes. Take the cinnamon out, and serve hot, with rice.

P can Pi (Unit d Stat s)

Pecan nuts are an important crop for farmers in the southern United States. They **export** them all over the world. Pecan nuts have a sweeter flavor than most nuts. Pecan pie is a popular traditional dish all over the United States. It is delicious warm or cold.

What you need

¼ cup (50 g) dark soft brown sugar
4 tbsp light syrup
1 tbsp butter
7 oz (200 g) pecan halves
1 egg
1 tsp vanilla
8-in. (20-cm) pie crust

What you do

1 Put the sugar, light syrup, and butter into a pan. Heat them very slowly over low heat until the butter has melted. Stir well and leave to cool.

2 **Preheat** the oven to 350°F (180°C).

3 Put the pie crust onto a baking sheet.

4 Scatter half the pecans over the crust, and level them. Arrange a circle of pecan halves around the edge of the pastry, and then another circle inside it. Keep making circles of nuts until you reach the center.

5 **Beat** the egg and the vanilla with a fork. Stir this into the cooled sugar mixture, and then pour the liquid over the pecan nuts.

6 **Bake** the pie for 30 minutes, or until the egg and sugar mixture has set in the center of the pie. Cool for 15 minutes.

7 Cut the pie into six slices, and serve with ice cream.

THE HISTORY OF PECAN PIE

In the late 17th century, French explorers settled in New Orleans, Louisiana. The Native Americans living there introduced them to the pecan nut. The French settlers invented pecan pie—a delicious way to enjoy the nuts.

Apple Pancakes (The Netherlands)

People in the Netherlands enjoy different kinds of pancakes. They might cook them with cheese, ham, or fruit. Dutch cooks mix the filling with the batter, and serve the pancake flat on a large plate. This recipe is particularly popular in the Netherlands.

What you need

3 oz (100 g) plain flour
2 tsp soft brown sugar
1 tsp **ground** cinnamon
¼ tsp ground cloves
1 egg
1 cup (200 ml) milk
1 red apple
1 green apple
4 tsp vegetable oil

What you do

1 **Sift** the flour, sugar, and ground spices into a bowl. Using a spoon, make a dip in the middle.

2 **Beat** the egg, add the milk, and beat again until well mixed. Pour the mixture into the dip in the flour, and gradually stir the liquid into the flour.

3 Beat the pancake batter well, and then put it aside. Turn the oven on to its lowest setting.

4 Use an apple corer to take the apple cores out.

5 Cut the apples in half, and then into thin **slices**. Stir the apple slices into the batter.

(!) 6 Heat ½ tsp oil in an 9-in. (23-cm) frying pan. Using a metal tablespoon, add 2 tbsp of pancake batter and apple slices to the pan. Tilt the pan to cover the bottom with batter.

7 Cook for 2–3 minutes over low to medium heat, until the pancake is golden brown on one side.

8 Use a spatula to flip the pancake over, and cook the other side. Lift the pancake onto a plate, put another plate on top, and keep it warm in the oven while you cook the rest of the batter in the same way.

9 Serve the pancakes hot, either on their own, or with a little maple syrup or ice cream.

Athol Brosse (Scotland)

Athol brosse means "broth, or thick soup, from Athol," which is an area in Scotland. The main ingredients are all produced in Scotland—oatmeal, honey, and raspberries. If you prefer, replace the cream with soy cream. Serve as a dessert, or as a cool treat on a hot day.

What you need

6 tbsp pinhead oatmeal

2 cups (460 ml) heavy cream

3 tbsp runny honey

1 cup (200 g) fresh raspberries

Sprigs of mint

What you do

1 Scatter the oatmeal on a baking tray.

2 Heat the oven **broiler** to medium. Put the baking tray under the broiler, and **broil** the oatmeal for about 1 minute, until the oatmeal starts to turn golden brown. Set it aside to cool.

3 Put the cream into a bowl. Using a handheld electric whisk or wire whisk, **whisk** the cream until it starts becoming firmer.

4 Spoon the honey over the cream.

5 Pour the oatmeal into the cream. Using a metal spoon, cut through the cream to **fold** the oatmeal in.

6 Keeping four raspberries aside, divide the rest into four glass bowls. Spoon the cream mixture on top of the raspberries.

7 Top each glass with a raspberry and a sprig of fresh mint.

8 Chill for 30 minutes before serving.

HEATHERY HONEY

Bees collect pollen from flowers to make into honey. The bees that make Scottish honey have gathered pollen from the heather that covers the hills and mountains of Scotland. Scots say that this makes their honey taste unlike any other kind.

Further Information

Here are some places to find out more about vegetarian food and cooking.

Cookbooks

Behnke, Alison. *Vegetarian Cooking Around the World.* Minneapolis: Lerner Publishing Group, 2002.

Braman, Arlette N. *Kids Around the World Cook!* New York: John Wiley & Sons, 2000.

Pratt, Dianne. *Hey Kids, You're Cookin' Now.* Chattanooga: Harvest Hill Press, 1998.

Vezza, Diane Simone. *Passport on a Plate.* New York: Simon & Schuster, 1997.

Wilkes, Angela. *Children's Step-by-Step Cookbook.* New York: DK Publishing, 2001.

Books for Vegetarians

Schwartz, Ellen. *I'm a Vegetarian: Amazing Facts and Ideas for Healthy Vegetarians.* Plattsburgh, N.Y.: Tundra Books of Northern New York, 2002.

Serafin, Kim. *Everything You Need to Know about Being Vegetarian.* New York: The Rosen Publishing Group, Inc., 1999.

Measurements and Conversions

3 teaspoons=1 tablespoon	1 tablespoon=½ fluid ounce	1 teaspoon=5 milliliters
4 tablespoons=¼ cup	1 cup=8 fluid ounces	1 tablespoon=15 milliliters
5 tablespoons=⅓ cup	1 cup=½ pint	1 cup=240 milliliters
8 tablespoons=½ cup	2 cups=1 pint	1 quart=1 liter
10 tablespoons=⅔ cup	4 cups=1 quart	1 ounce=28 grams
12 tablespoons=¾ cup	2 pints=1 quart	1 pound=454 grams
16 tablespoons=1 cup	4 quarts=1 gallon	

Healthy Eating

This diagram shows which foods you should eat to stay healthy. Most of your food should come from the bottom of the pyramid. Eat some of the foods from the middle every day. Only eat a little of the foods from the tip. Although the pyramid recommends meat, being a vegetarian does not mean you cannot eat a healthy, balanced diet. Most of the foods we need to stay healthy are in the middle and bottom of this pyramid, which do not include any meat at all. Vegetarians should eat some foods from the top middle layer as well, such as **legumes**, nuts, and milk.

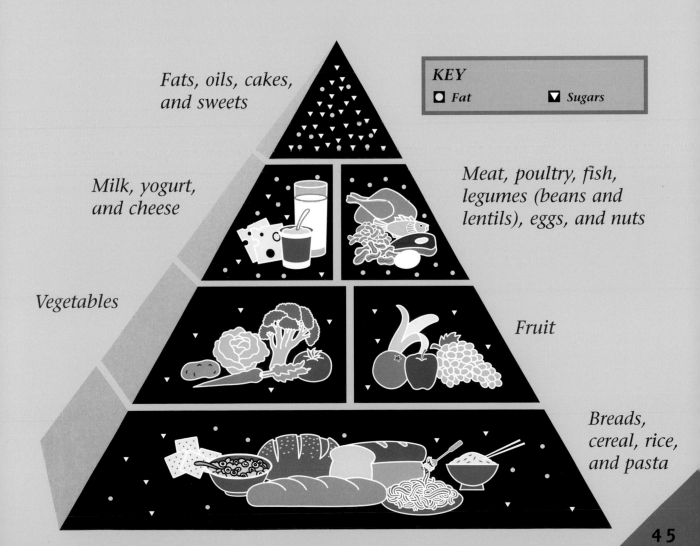

Fats, oils, cakes, and sweets

KEY
◻ Fat　　　▽ Sugars

Milk, yogurt, and cheese

Meat, poultry, fish, legumes (beans and lentils), eggs, and nuts

Vegetables

Fruit

Breads, cereal, rice, and pasta

Glossary

bake cook something in the oven

beat mix ingredients together, using a fork or whisk

blend mix ingredients together in a blender or food processor

boil cook a liquid on the stove. Boiling liquid bubbles and steams.

breed mate animals for the purpose of feeding people

broil cook under the broiler in the oven

calcium mineral in foods, such as milk and cheese, that helps us grow strong teeth and bones

chill put a dish into the refrigerator for a while before serving

chop cut into pieces using a sharp knife

chutney a spicy sauce served with curries. Chutneys often contain chopped fruits and vegetables.

cover put a lid on a pan, or put foil or plastic wrap over a dish

deep-fry cook in a deep pan of hot oil

drain remove liquid, usually by pouring something into a colander or sieve

dressing sauce for a salad

dry-fry fried in a pan without any oil

export to sell a product to another country

fold mixing wet and dry ingredients by making cutting movements with a metal spoon

fondue set utensils used for melting cheese

fry cook something in oil in a pan

garnish decorate food, for example, with fresh herbs

grate break something, such as cheese, into small pieces using a grater

ground made into a fine powder

knead press and fold with the hands

legume beans, peas, or seeds from plants that often have pods

mash crush a food until it is soft and pulpy

nutrient substance that provides nourishment

peel remove the skin of a fruit or vegetable

pita bread flat, unrisen bread

preheat turn on the oven in advance, so that it is hot when you want to use it

protein a natural substance in food that our bodies need to stay healthy

sift remove lumps from dry ingredients, such as flour, with a sieve

simmer cook liquid on the stove. Simmering liquid bubbles and steams gently.

slice cut ingredients into thin, flat pieces

staple one of the most important foods in a person's diet

thawed no longer frozen

toast heat under a broiler or in a toaster

vegan person who does not eat any food that has come from an animal, including milk and eggs

vegetarian food that does not contain meat. People who do not eat meat are called vegetarians.

vitamins natural chemicals in food that the body uses to stay healthy

whisk mix ingredients using a wire whisk

Index